Parasites on the outside of the body are just as easily removed. Like ticks, most can be pulled out of the skin. The war on parasites has begun!

"Come at me, parasites. **I HAVE TWEEZERS!**"

CREATURE COMBAT

Even inside our bodies, a parasite can still be beaten. Doctors can give us medicines that kill it or help us get rid of it naturally.

"So, this is what 'naturally' means..."

TICKS

Not all parasites steal the host's food like the tongue-eating louse does. Ticks are very small <u>arachnids</u> that feed on their host's blood.

"ARGH! Vampire parasites! RUN!"

The barnacle then takes over the crab's entire body, including its brain. It turns the crab into a big babysitter for its newly hatched parasite babies.

"It can control the crab's brain? Not cool, barnacle. Not cool."

SACCULINA CARCINI

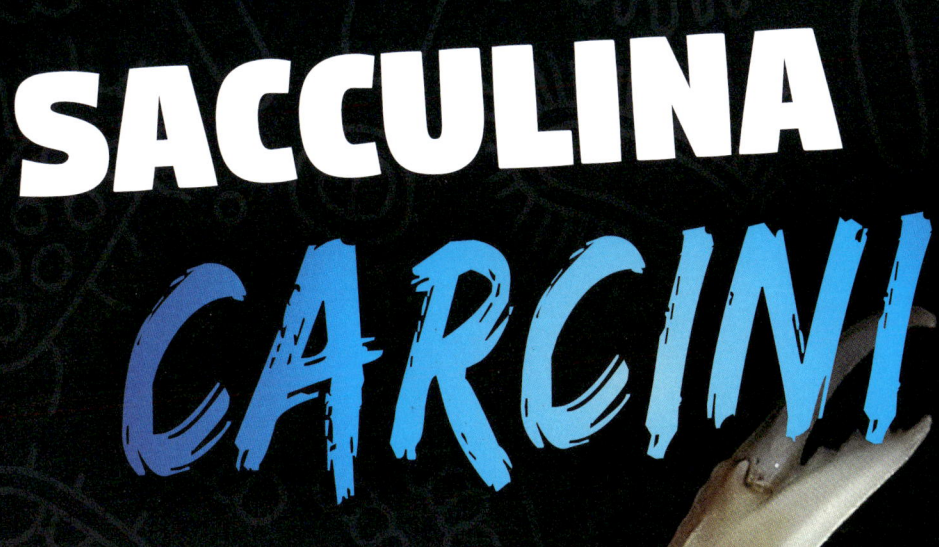

Some parasites can completely control their host. Sacculina carcini is a <u>barnacle</u> that latches onto a crab and lays its eggs inside the crab's shell.

"Crabs are NOT puppets! Leave them alone, barnacle."

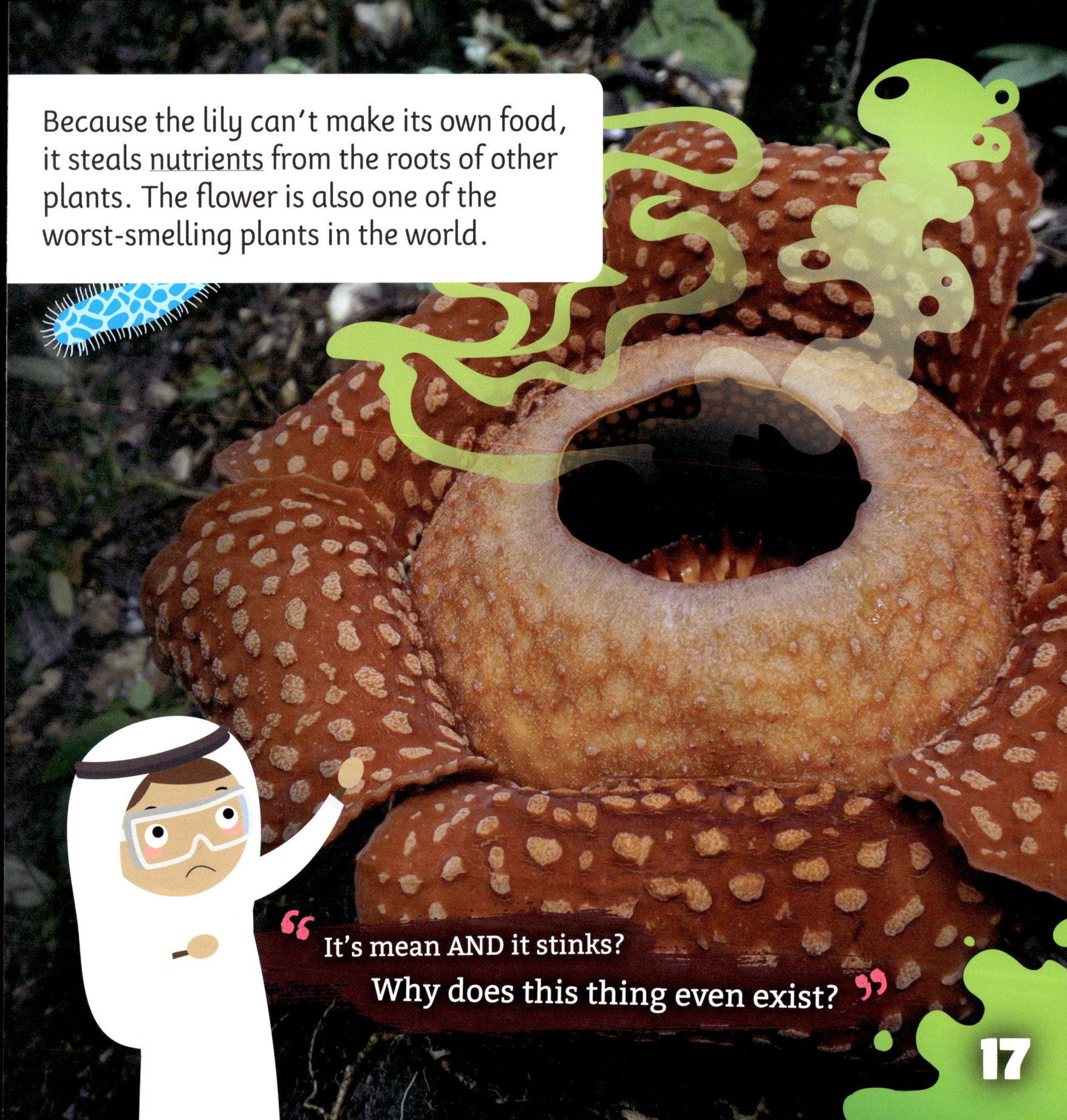

Because the lily can't make its own food, it steals <u>nutrients</u> from the roots of other plants. The flower is also one of the worst-smelling plants in the world.

"It's mean AND it stinks? Why does this thing even exist?"

GREEN-BANDED BROODSAC

The green-banded broodsac parasite turns snails into zombies to help it complete its life cycle.

"It's like we're living in a scary film!"

Tapeworms can have all sorts of bad effects on humans. They can cause:

- Tummy pain
- Diarrhoea (runny poo)
- Vomiting
- Feeling more, or less, hungry
- Weight loss

"Thank goodness these things are rare..."

TAPEWORMS

Humans are targets for parasites too. Tapeworms are a type of parasite that live in your intestines. Some tapeworms can be many metres long.

"I think I need to lie down."

TONGUE-EATING LOUSE

All sorts of living things can be attacked by parasites. Some fish have to live with the tongue-eating louse.

"I... I can see its head! GROSS!"

Some parasites are too small for us to see and others can be gigantic. No matter the size, they can cause the host a lot of harm.

"Parasites sound awful. They just take, take, take. **SO SELFISH!**"

Taking the host's food helps parasites to grow before they <u>reproduce</u>. This starts the parasite's <u>life cycle</u> again.

"They multiply? ONE WAS ENOUGH!"

PESKY PARASITES

A parasite is a creature that lives in or on another living thing, called the host. Parasites need a host in order to survive.

> "Does that hurt the host?"

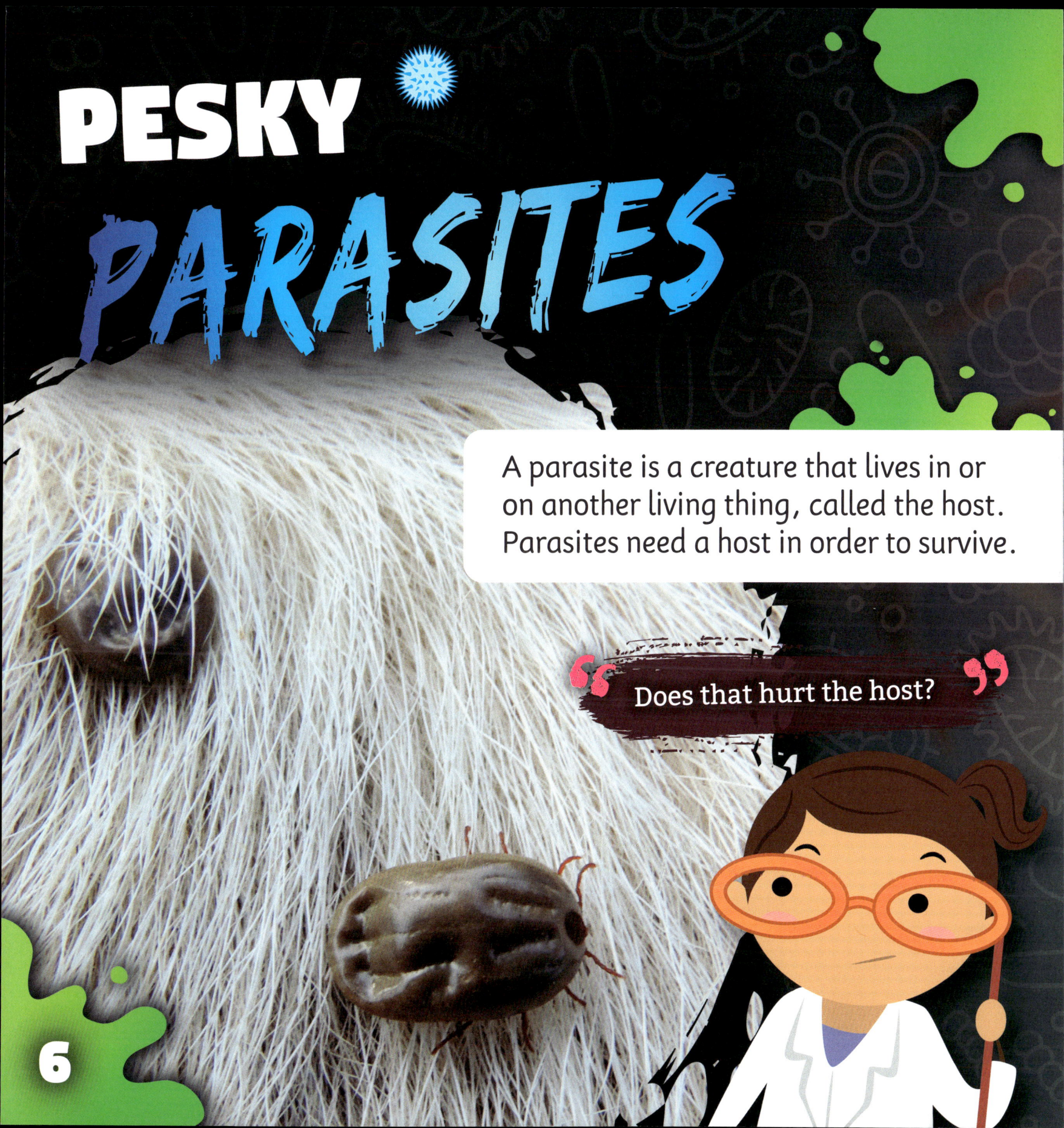

There are some things that live in and on us that are big enough to see. Some of these creatures can even be many metres long.

"METRES? Well, I won't be needing my microscope for those..."

LITTLE AND LARGE

Many microorganisms are so small that we can't even see them. These tiny terrors live in and on our bodies, and we usually don't even know they're there.

"Micro means tiny. Organism means a living thing."

CONTENTS

PAGE 4	Little and Large
PAGE 6	Pesky Parasites
PAGE 10	Tongue-Eating Louse
PAGE 12	Tapeworms
PAGE 14	Green-Banded Broodsac
PAGE 16	Corpse Lily
PAGE 18	Sacculina Carcini
PAGE 20	Ticks
PAGE 22	Creature Combat
PAGE 24	Glossary and Index

Words that look like this can be found in the glossary on page 24.

TRICKY WORDS

PARASITE = singular (one parasite)
PARASITES = plural (many parasites)
PARASITIC = to do with a parasite or many parasites

BookLife PUBLISHING

©This edition published 2023.
First published 2019.
BookLife Publishing Ltd.
King's Lynn
Norfolk, PE30 4LS
ISBN: 978-1-78637-829-3
ISBN: 978-1-80155-925-6

Written by:
William Anthony

Edited by:
Madeline Tyler

Designed by:
Amy Li

A catalogue record for this book is available from the British Library.

All rights reserved. Printed in Poland.

All facts, statistics, web addresses and URLs in this book were verified as valid and accurate at time of writing. No responsibility for any changes to external websites or references can be accepted by either the author or publisher.

PHOTO CREDITS

All images courtesy of Shutterstock. With thanks to Getty Images, Thinkstock Photo and iStockphoto.

Used throughout (including cover) – chekart (background), Sonechko57 (slime), VectorShow (microbe characters), Alena Ohneva (vector microbes), Olga_C (circle image frame). Used throughout (excluding cover) – Photo Melon (clipboard), Lorelyn Medina (scientist characters). P4–5 – Yurchanka Siarhei, Rattiya Thongdumhyu, p6–7 – SNP_SS, svtdesign, p8–9 – Crevis, Rattiya Thongdumhyu, p10–11 – Francesco_Ricciardi, Ayah Raushan, Crystal Eye Studio, chanawutt13, CloudyStock, p12–13 – Juan Gaertner, yusufdemirci, p14–15 – Henri Koskinen, Pavel1964, mark smith nsb, Christoph Burgstedt, p16–17 – Lano La, Yana Alisovna, p18–19 – jiraphoto, Hans Hillewaert, p20–21 – Aksenova Natalya, vectopicta, p23–24 – Monkey Business Images, motorolka, Sudowoodo.

ATTACK OF THE... PESKY PARASITES

By William Anthony